ENCORE
CHURCH

What makes people *come back*?

WAYNE CORDEIRO

The Encore Church
Copyright © 2009
Wayne Cordeiro

 Published by Life Resources
290 Sand Island Access Road
Honolulu, HI 96819

Cover design by Larry Ganiron
Hawaiian Church Illustration by Clairelane Yoshioka

Unless otherwise identified, Scripture quotations are taken from the *NEW AMERICAN STANDARD BIBLE*, © Copyright the Lockman Foundation 1960, 1962, 1963, 1968, 1971, 1972, 1973, 1975, 1977, 1995. Used by permission. (www.Lockman.org)

Scripture quotations identified NIV are from the HOLY BIBLE, NEW INTERNATIONAL VERSION® Copyright © 1973, 1978, 1984 by International Bible Society. Used by permission of Zondervan Publishing House. All rights reserved.

All rights reserved. No part of this publication may be reproduced, stored in a retrieval system, or transmitted in any form or by any means—electronic, mechanical, photocopying, recording, or otherwise—without the prior written permission of the publisher. The only exception is brief quotations in printed reviews.

Published by Life Resources
290 Sand Island Access Road
Honolulu, HI 96819

Printed in the United State of America

Library of Congress Cataloging-in-Publication Data

Cordeiro, Wayne
    The Encore Church

Summary: "A collection of qualities that make up an Encore Church. These qualities, while not an exhaustive list, are quintessential to churches that plan to indelibly influence their communities."

ISBN 1-929351-20-8

Mahalo

Thank you to the following people who have contributed so much to making New Hope Oahu an *Encore Church:*

Greg and Annie Kemp
Ray and Sherel Stosik
Charlie and Kathy Thurston
Glenn and Garleen Umetsu

You constantly remind us of what commitment can accomplish.

It is an understatement to say how much I appreciate all the people it takes to be an *Encore Church.* Our directional team makes ministry fun: **John Tilton, Tim Savage, Elwin Ahu, Mike Sharpe, Rod Shimabukuro,** and **Aaron Cordeiro**.

I so appreciate those who assist me and are much smarter than I am in everything: **Mary Waialeale, Ann Young,** and **Cindy Goo**. I am also thankful for the stellar team led by **Rauna May** and **Amy Sugawa** who do the painstaking task of proofreading. Scattered thoughts go in one end and literary prose comes out the other. You make me look much better than I really am.

Our Church council has been more than partners. They have become friends along the way: **Greg Kemp, Murray Hohns, Glenn Ogasawara, Ray Stosik, Russell Luke, Dayne Kaneshiro,** and **Dave Sorensen**. When I wrestled with my health, they were like Aaron and Hur alongside of Moses, holding his hands up until victory was achieved.

You are the very kind of people who bring life to an Encore Church.

Dedication

This book is dedicated to two brides:

One is my dear wife **Anna** who for thirty-five years has always reminded me that it is only through love that lives are changed—mine included.

The other is the Bride of Christ, the **Church** … one expression in particular, **New Hope Oahu**—a network of radiant and joyful servants who embody the definition of grace and beauty in these islands.

Preface

It has taken me twenty-five years to write this book.

I'm not necessarily a slow writer. It's simply because these irreducible principles become recognizable only after the passing of decades. They are garnered along the way: easily found, but often quickly lost. After twenty-five years of ministry in Hawaii, I have taken the time to capture and catalogue them in this book ... those certain markings that incline people either to freshness or to musty living.

In this beautiful archipelago of islands, *hana hou* is the Hawaiian word for *encore!* We shout that after an extraordinary performance or whenever we want something to continue and never end.

People are not tired of the gospel. They are simply tired of tired presentations of the gospel—whether it is presented over a pulpit or through an individual's life.

And it is precisely here, the veracity of the gospel will be ultimately measured.

What you are about to read is a collection of qualities that make up an *Encore Church*. These are not exhaustive by any means, but these qualities are quintessential to churches that plan to indelibly influence their communities.

The qualities we are about to highlight apply equally to the qualities of an encore life. Why? It is because a church is not a building. It is made up of individual lives, and collectively we comprise what the Bible calls the Church, the Bride of Christ.

What you are is what She is.

A SPIRIT OF GRATEFULNESS

Here is where we begin our journey together.
But before you start reading, ask God to weave these
qualities into the fabric of your soul. It will be the best
contribution you can make to the Church.

*E*ver pull over and stop long enough to breathe in a morning's sunrise?

When was the last time you saw elephant shapes in the clouds? We hardly do that anymore, without guilt anyway. The day's demands beckon us. Surrender to those demands and you will miss the eternal. Life will not be rushed and it is only in pausing that we develop gratefulness.

An old rabbinic saying I heard years ago still haunts me:

> **"God will one day hold us each accountable for all the things He created for us to enjoy, but we refused to do so."** [1]

The first mark of an *Encore Church* is *gratefulness*.

I am learning that a spirit of gratefulness can only be developed when I pause to notice a rainbow or refuse to rush past a sunset. When I take the time to notice, I feel arising in me a *deep appreciation* that wasn't there before. I am again reminded that I have: breath in my lungs, good friends, and for-giveness—all things I've never deserved but have been granted nonetheless.

I believe God is more concerned about us being grateful than just about anything else.

STOP SIGNS

Sometimes God sends us a divine directive to be still so He can restore us once again. He intentionally removes the hurry from our step in order for us to correct our cadence.

It happened to me recently when I received a *mulligan from God*. After several months of chest pains, I was diagnosed with having three blockages in my heart. I was put on the next plane to Stanford Medical Center in California. Four days later, after a successful surgery, I took a detour to our family farm in Oregon to recuperate. There my two daughters, son-in-law, and two grandchildren live happily alongside thirteen chickens, three dogs, four cats, and one cow.

One of my favorite seasons is autumn. Misty mornings segue into sunny afternoons. I enjoy the chilly, invigorating dawns that eventually surrender to soft rays that creep up and gently warm you.

My blood count was still low, so I tired easily. But I was being ordered to *still my soul* and simply be *grateful* I was alive. I slowed my tempo and took in the moment on that early October morning as I drove to a nearby coffee shop for devotions.

A morning fog lay shrouded on the meadows like soft cotton. Circling the surrounding hills, a wispy haze created the appearance of a passing train that left in its wake a disappearing trail of steam. Then like a slow, rising curtain, the receding fog revealed a choir of verdant cedars, reminding me of the 98th Psalm: *"Let the mountains sing together for joy."*[2]

The sun's spotlight introduced the morning scene.

The fog danced in individual ribbons on the surface of a nearby lake. It resembled a hundred tiny mystical fairies celebrating the opening act in the dawning sunlight. I was transported back to Camelot visualizing the Lady of the Lake rising out of a haunting mist.

Sunlit dew outlined intricate spider webs adorning the pine trees along our driveway, and smaller webs appeared as snowy ornaments suspended from the upper branches.

The ospreys were in flight that day. They have such a majestic and haunting presence gliding high above the farm. They approached the nearby lake, as their market of choice, to garner an unlucky fish or two for their hatchlings.

It is early fall at our family farm, but that morning, it was the opening act of a divine musical that displayed God's splendor. **The majesty of God was all around me.** I found myself grateful and renewed.

FINDING HIM CLOSE

God's artistry is not limited to the beauty of a rural countryside. It is evident everywhere … if we will only stop to notice. **Gratefulness is only discovered when you remove all hurry from your life.**

Listen …

I heard His delight in my granddaughter's laughter. I sensed His pleasure in the gathering of God's people this past weekend. I heard Him sigh with satisfaction in the rustling of the palm trees near our home and I was once again so grateful. I must never tire of being overwhelmed by His artistry.

The first mark of an *Encore Church* is a spirit of gratefulness.

New Hope Oahu had its humble beginnings thirteen years ago. We haven't been graced with a permanent building yet, so at a local high school, one team sets up and another takes down after five services. At nine other locations, the same scenario is repeated. New Hope requires the involvement of 1500 volunteers every weekend just so we can have church!

We have become one family in many locations, linked together by a common heart for Christ, a love for one another, and a video link. Along with ten other daughter churches, we comprise a constellation of colleagues to reach these beautiful islands with the news of God's love.

Although we don't have what others may, we are yet grateful. Land prices have skyrocketed. One acre of Hawaii real estate is appraised at 2.5 million dollars. We would require a minimum of 20 acres; so with a little math, we would require 50 million dollars just for starters. Even at those prices, finding 20 contiguous acres available anywhere near Honolulu would border on the miraculous.

We can either complain about what we do not have, or we can be grateful for what we have.

We have chosen the latter.

Gratefulness differs from thankfulness. Of course, both are essential. But thankfulness can be defined as the cordial response to a favor done. It is the affirmation you give when things go your way. It is the reply to a gift or a promotion; it's the *hooray* after a blessing.

Gratefulness, however, is different. It can only be developed intentionally. It begins with a spirit. It's an attitude, a disposition that we carry whether or not things go our way. It's being content before any gifts are given. It's breathing a *silent* "thank you" regardless of what the circumstances are. It's the *hallelujah* with no guarantee of a blessing. It is the confidence to accept whatever God brings.

New Hope is not a church for younger people nor is it a church for the elderly. It is a gathering for all whom Christ has chosen to invite, and we have decided that we will have little or no say in the matter. We simply receive those who come, whether they arrive in three-piece suits or in wheelchairs. He has asked us to welcome them. *We simply receive all those who come.*

It was on the heels of a rousing worship service when individual voices cried out, "Yes, Lord!" Then from the far rear of the sanctuary, a raspy voice raised, "Yes, Lord!" From the front, another exclamation rang out, "Yes, Lord!" After several more, the pastor quieted his exuberant congregation and said, "Brethren, let us pray." They bowed their heads in silence as the pastor raised his voice. "Lord!" he cried. "You have heard our answer in *advance!* Ask whatever You may and our answer still remains, *"Yes, Lord!"*

Gratefulness is our hearts before the blessing. *"Yes"* is our answer before His requests. Gratefulness helps us to see what others cannot and appreciate what others would not.

EYES THAT SEE

In Matthew 6:22-23, Jesus said, "The eye is the lamp of the body; so then if your eye is clear, your whole body will be full of light. But if your eye is bad, your whole body will be full of darkness."[3]

Jesus is referring to how we perceive life. It is how we choose to see things. One paints things darkly while another paints them bright. It defines the *colors on our palette.* One person's tray holds only grays while another's bounces with neon colors. We choose how we will paint situations, setbacks, and circumstances.

❧ What colors will you use? ❧

Gratefulness searches for splendor. It takes the time to see the grandeur in the simple. It respects the wisdom that's etched into every line in an elder's countenance. It looks past the pierced lip and searches for the potential within a young ruffian. *Every stroke of the brush must be intentional if you are to paint a masterpiece.*

EARS THAT HEAR

It is said that toward the end of his days, the legendary Beethoven became deaf. The portals that once enchanted his soul were silenced by age. Yet he played. Following the composition, his fingers awakened symphonies only he could imagine. To any normal ear, the music coming from his worn-out piano sounded discordant and dissonant; yet tears would stream down the cheeks of the famed composer as he played.[4] Why?

Beethoven was hearing the music the piano should make, not what it did make.

Gratefulness is the Beethoven of our churches. It is the portals through which our days may dance again. It hears the sounds of what could be, and it guides us with hope. It reminds us of all the gifts that we should not have been given, the friends we do not deserve, and the grace we did not earn.

It is easy to lose this fragile gift. It is readily displaced or unwittingly exchanged for *want*. It slumps into entitlement and tricks us into thinking that we deserve more than we do.

Instead, gratefulness is to be *cherished* and carefully maintained. It is to be exercised in the shadows as well as in the footlights; *equally* in the extravagant as in the common.

One of the habits Anna and I have is to periodically remind each other to be grateful. I recall when we bought our first home, a 780 square foot house. It wasn't much, but we would often comment to one another after returning from a long day: "What a beautiful home we have!" Of course, it wouldn't attract any interest from *Better Homes and Gardens,* but we were grateful nevertheless. It was more about the *condition of our hearts* than it was the condition of our house.

Each weekend, I drive onto the high school campus where New Hope has held their weekend services for over a decade. I notice the many tents that have been set up the night before. I see our parking attendants who have arrived at 5 AM and other volunteers who have helped transform the school's seventy-year-old auditorium, once slated for demolition, into a palace fit for the King. Tears blur my eyes and I am once again reminded of the *treasure* we have in our midst. We couldn't do church without them.

All our receptionists at New Hope are volunteers. It's been that way since our inception. One dear lady has been volunteering every Wednesday for over four years. Approaching the front desk, I stopped to acknowledge her faithfulness and to thank her for taking her only day off to answer phones and greet visitors.

"Oh no!" she replied. "I should thank you!" she said. "I look forward to this all week long. This is where my soul finds rest and my heart is uplifted!"

Just ask our volunteers sometime about their ministry, and they will gush with gratefulness.

I pray that the eyes of your heart may
be enlightened, so that you will know ... the riches of the
glory of His inheritance in the saints and what is
the surpassing greatness of His power.[5]
(Ephesians 1:18-19)

LIVING HEART FIRST

*L*in Miaoke is a beautiful nine-year-old girl who was in the opening ceremonies of the 2008 Olympics in Beijing. She belted out *"Ode to the Motherland"* to the applause of the world. We've since discovered that she was not singing. She was only performing. The real singer was seven-year-old Yang Peiyi, hidden behind stage because her appearance didn't make the final cut. Yang Peiyi is still getting her front teeth in so they're not perfect. Most seven-year-olds would be able to relate, but Chinese officials pulled her from the stage because a Communist party official decided her looks were not *suitable.*

Spokeswoman for the Olympic organizing committee, Sun Weide, explained, "We decided to let Lin Miaoke sing on stage and use Yang Peiyi's voice, because Yang Peiyi has the *best voice* while Lin Miaoke is the *best actress*.

That was a nice spin; but when you think about it, best actress is actually a thin euphemism for *best image.* Of course, we surely do not blame either of the young girls, but it does perpetuate the myth that a Hollywood-esque image is everything. The illusion is that if we look good, then we must be good.

Right?

Wrong!

WHAT GOD STILL USES

In the pioneer days of New Hope, all we had was *heart.* We didn't have chairs; we sat on cafeteria tables. We didn't have instruments; every musician had to bring his own. But we had heart and that is all God needed to begin.

We'd set up a gauntlet of greeters, eight on each side; and when people arrived, they were funneled between our grandstands of huggers. We would later be coined the *hugging church*, known for converging on anything within ten feet.

We sang with all our hearts. We served with all our hearts. We set up and took down with all our hearts, and the church grew and grew.

I remember praying in the early days of New Hope: *"God, I pray that one day we will have our own chairs, our own sound system, and maybe even some paid staff with our own office!"*

I didn't mind working out of my briefcase at a coffee shop, but it wasn't long before our discipleship groups were taking up the dining area. The store manager kindly asked us to find a larger venue, shrink our influence, or buy out the coffee shop.

As the months passed by, we saved enough money to rent our own office space. We bought our own chairs and purchased our own musical instruments! We had our own sound system and even bought our *own* vans.

We had arrived!

One day, however, a lady's innocent comment returned me to what was most important. She remarked, "I love the music and I love the drama. We have talented musicians and such wonderful services. I remember the early days when we had little or nothing, yet we thrived. We had heart. We used to have such big hearts. I am sure it's still there, but it's hard to see anymore. *Where's the heart?"*

And she was right. During this last season, we had flat-lined. We began new programs and new initiatives. Completion of tasks and results became more important than anything else. Although the heart of New Hope was still present, it was no longer *emphasized.* That night I spent extra time in prayer asking for God's counsel.

I honestly cannot tell you that this was an audible voice, but I knew it was His instruction nevertheless. Paraphrasing, I heard Him say:

"Correct back to the heart. Peel away whatever you need to until the servant's hearts are once again visible. In the end, a mind will reach a mind, but only a heart will reach a heart."

God directed us to reemphasize the importance of our hearts. That is what God used to grow our church then, and it is what God would use to grow our church now.

And so we did.

We pruned any program or task that relied more on image than heart. We culled initiatives that were based on talent more than on character and no sacred cows were safe.

We restructured until we could see the light of genuine hearts again.

BOTH / AND

By the way, I am not suggesting that competency isn't important. *Heart and excellence* are not mutually exclusive. In other words, it is not an *either-or.* It is a *both-and.* A common tendency is to use heart as an excuse for being sloppy. But when we live heart first, excellence usually follows.

It is true that God has not asked us to be successful; He has asked us to be faithful. But sometimes the reason we are not successful is because we have not been faithful.

The *Encore Church* may have some crooked teeth and not everyone may sing in perfect pitch, but that's not what keeps people away. It's when the image wears away and they see that we've been lip-syncing. That is when everything loses its luster.

Living heart first does not come accidentally. It is maintained only by vigilant monitoring. Human tendency always drifts toward selfishness, and only through a conscious, daily effort will we break free from it.

THREE CHARACTERISTICS

You can spot people who live heart first. They are *quicker to forgive.* They overlook flaws and crooked teeth. They see people over an image, enjoy each other, and are more prone to laughter. Formal programs are less necessary in order for something to happen.

People who live heart first also have a larger capacity to *receive correction.* They welcome improvement even though it is delivered by unconventional means—a child, a boss, a mother or father, an in-law, a critic.

And people who live heart first live a *surrendered life.* Mother Teresa, one of my heroes, taught me much about the surrendered heart. Before she died in 1997, she directed the Missionaries of Charity where she ministered for over 45 years. A Nobel Peace Prize recipient, she worked with those who had contracted HIV/AIDS, leprosy, and tuberculosis. Her Catholic order ran soup kitchens, children's and family counseling programs, orphanages, and schools.

Malcolm Muggeridge wrote of this modern day saint in his wonderful documentary, *Something Beautiful for God.* In it, her humility is as bright as her eloquence:

In this life we cannot do great things. We can only do small things with great love.[1]

DULY REMINDED

Several years ago New Hope held a talent night. We gathered our brightest and best on stage for an evening of concert and drama rich in ambience. From the opening presentation, the full house of enthusiasts knew this would be an evening to remember. Brilliant dances, extraordinary solos, enchanting dramas, and beautiful choreography graced the stage. I sat spellbound realizing how endowed we were as a church.

Just toward the end of the evening, the lights dimmed and one of our special children appeared on stage. Nikki has Down syndrome. She and her parents began attending the church when we first started in a junior high school cafeteria. She appeared confident and convinced that she was supposed to be there ... except for the fact that she wasn't sure *why!*

A few awkward seconds passed when Darlene Zs-chech's song, "Lord I Give You My Heart" spilled over the sound system. Using American Sign Language, Nikki began. Her hand motions and demeanor found increasing confidence with each passing lyric, reminding us of the One who gave His life. I felt myself drawn to the *truth* of this re-minder and as I surrendered to it, *I felt something deep down being* **recalibrated.**

The anthem concluded. With hands upraised, she stood empty ... held together only by His pleasure. All activity in heaven seemed stilled for the moment.

Overcome with emotion, tears and audible sobs overpowered our good manners and we broke into a standing ovation with shouts of *"Encore!"*

That evening found us gathered together before the throne to remind us of what God delighted in the most.

Watch over your heart with all diligence,
for from it flow the springs of life.[2]
(Proverbs 4:23)

THE PRESENCE OF GOD

*N*ew Hope is a mobile church. The cost and availability of land in Hawaii has kept us *homeless* for over thirteen years. But it would not be opulent facilities but the *presence of God* that would make our gatherings sparkle.

I have always been an avid student of the hand of God. I have seen His *favor* rest on one church and pass over another. I have witnessed His *hand* on a ministry for decades and I have seen it lift off another after only a few months. I have seen some chase after His *blessings* and never catch up; and for others, I have watched His blessings overwhelm them! I remember Moses declaring: "All these blessings will come upon you and overtake you if you obey the Lord your God."[1] (Deuteronomy 28:2)

It was during the Welsh Revival in 1904 under the teaching of Evan Roberts. A hungry enthusiast traveling to experience the revival disembarked in South Wales. As he left the platform, he asked the conductor, *"Do you know the location of the church where the revival is taking place?"*

The conductor simply replied, *"Just start walking. It will find you."*[2]

SINGING IN THE RAIN

I remember one February some years ago. We were notified that the high school auditorium we used each weekend would not be available in six weeks. These notices for us to find an auxiliary facility usually came six to eight months in advance due to the logistics of relocating the sheer size of

10,000 people.

Profuse with apologies, the school handed us the memo. We understood that we had the gargantuan task of finding another spot for our weekend services in only six weeks.

We began knocking on doors. We tried our local Aloha Stadium, public halls, the university, and any place large enough to hold 10,000 people. But nothing was available; nothing ... except our last option—*an outdoor park.* The dilemma was that our Hawaiian weather is usually uncooperative during the spring months. One day it's blue skies; the next is pelting rain.

But we had no other choice. We reserved the park and initiated an emergency prayer program to persuade God to keep the skies blue ... at least for one weekend.

As the time approached, we made our preparations. We rented a larger-than-life sound system, hundreds of lights, and multiple staging. Our plan was to hold three services instead of our regular five—one late Saturday afternoon and two on Sunday morning.

The tent to protect the stage looked like a gigantic airplane hangar and another tent, sufficient to hold about 1000, was erected. The others would have to sit under the canopy of the stars at night and, hopefully, blue skies in the morning.

The weekend approached with unfriendly signs of gray. Our first service began Saturday at 6 PM. A light drizzle leaked through, but we remained steady. The service concluded with most of us a bit damp but agreeable.

Before retiring that evening, I thought it wise to meet with the Chief Weatherman and log my concerns. My respectful plea began: *"Lord, You know how I've served you faithfully for lo' these many years. I have not asked of Thee long life nor for the life of mine enemies.* (When I get serious, I tend

to use the 1611 language of the King James era.)
*I beseech Thee for sunshine on this Thy beloved
people who shall gather in the morn that we might
praise Thee ... un-wetted.*"

Satisfied with my supplication and mastery of biblical languages, I drifted off to sleep.

The following morning, I was awakened by the sounds of pelting rain. Quickly I got back on my knees and this time, I spoke plainly: *"Dear God.
We can't have this! Singing in the rain might make
for a good musical, but it doesn't make for good
church services. God, turn off the faucet ... pul-
eeze!"*

Mustering up all the confidence I could, I walked toward my car *believing, in faith, with devoted as-
surance* ... that by the time I would get to the park, the rain would have abated. I drove out from our covered parking garage and as I entered the street, raindrops attacked my windshield. Unfettered, I drove onward, refusing to activate the windshield

wipers ... *in faith, believing* that it was clear skies. But all that did was make it hard to see the road.

By the time I arrived, the worship portion of the service had already begun. Like a saturated sponge, a huddled handful of faithful followers were *singing in the rain.* I joined them. Our postures were identical, but the content was not. With outstretched hands I raised up not hymns, but protests of complaint.

"God!" I objected, *"May I remind You again just how long I have been serving You? And I ask for one favor ... just one insignificant favor! And what do I get? I can't believe this."*

I remember His voice. It wasn't an angry voice, but it was firm. I don't know if anyone else heard it; but for me, it parted the heavens.

"You are more concerned with the absence of rain than you are about the presence of God."

That's all I heard. But everything stopped, or at least it seemed that way. The music stilled and the sweeping hand of time ground to a halt.

Those words yet echo in me till this day. I remember crying out for His presence and my concern about the rain paled in comparison. God was right. Without His presence, sun drenched beaches would result only in parched landscapes; but with *His presence, even a rainy morning could be the beginning of a revival that **transforms** the islands.*

We continued the service with a *renewed* heart for *His manifest presence.* By the end of our time together, the skies had parted and the most beautiful sunshine bathed His people with the affirmation of His attendance.

One man quipped, "You can take the Holy Spirit out of half the churches in America and they would keep right on going as if nothing happened."

That cannot be … especially in these last days. It is

the *Encore Church* that covets His presence *more* than facilities, more than stellar programs, more than notoriety or money.

Abraham Lincoln was not only a great president; he was a man of God. He would pray differently than most. Most Christian speakers before ascending to the podium are likely to pray: "Without You, Lord, I will fail." Abraham Lincoln would instead pray, "Without You, Lord … I *must* fail."[3]

It was a dangerous prayer, but it was an honest one.

He was aware that even as Christians we could muster up our human capabilities to carry out religious activities. He saw secularists, who had no inklings toward God, become successful in the eyes of their peers; their businesses would flourish with lucrative trade. And he knew that capable and shrewd Christians could do the same.

WHEN GOD SHOWS UP

I have witnessed the *hand of God* in sometimes obvious and, at other times, inconspicuous ways. Since the beginning of New Hope, we have baptized over 14,000 people at our local Ala Moana beach. Each time we have gathered at the ocean's shores, the Lord has never ceased to part the clouds and allow the sun to shine regardless of the time of year.

Once when we were praying for the baptism candidates, we were huddled under umbrellas in the pouring rain. But as soon as our short trek to the water began, the showers halted and a circle of sunshine spotlighted the event as if heaven were revealing to us a hint of God's delight. Our staff still talks about that day.

In Matthew 18:20, God promises to be in our midst: "For where two or three have gathered together in My name, I am there in their midst.⁴ Moreover, something miraculous takes place when we not only invoke His presence ... but when we live in such a way that honors Him.

And reticent of being overly dramatic, I hesitate to share this, but there have been many weekends where a *visible mist lingers* inside the auditorium as God's Word is spoken. I have had to blink to be sure it's not my contact lenses fogging over. I've never spoken publicly about it. I simply continue onward with a *warmer* sense of His gentle presence.

Sometimes He shouts; sometimes He is quiet.
And I am again reminded of Zephaniah's words:
"The Lord your God is in your midst ... He will exult over
you with joy, He will be quiet in His love."[5]
(Zephaniah 3:17)

HEALTHY RELATIONSHIPS

*I*t was in 2002 when I first understood the importance of healthy relationships.

I was conducting a leadership seminar in a Midwestern town. Following the sessions, I stayed an extra day to meet with a local board whose church was navigating a pastoral transition. While preparing for my meeting, I was in a restaurant having breakfast. Suddenly a man in his early thirties slid into the booth directly across from me.

"You're Wayne Cordeiro!"

"Last time I checked," I said with a slight smile, trying to look unsurprised.

"I'm a new pastor. Our church has flat-lined. I need some resources. You have a new book? A new tape? Maybe some fresh ideas for leaders like me?"

This time I laughed audibly. "Hold on," I said. "What's happening?"

"Our church needs help. We're *stuck*. We've tried dozens of new programs and spent thousands on conferences. But there isn't *any* program, no matter how much I hype it, that seems to work. They all die!"

He had my attention, so I pressed him further. "How long have you been the pastor?"

"Nine months," he replied.

"That's not a long time, but enough time to give

birth," I quipped. "How did you come to pastor this church anyway?"

He began slowly, choosing his words more carefully. "It wasn't good," he said shaking his head. "Our last pastor just up and left."

"Tell me about it." He had my attention.

"It was on a Sunday. He walked up to the pulpit. I thought he was about to begin his message; but instead he said, 'Could I have the elders stand?' One-by-one, the seven elders stood. The pastor then said, 'It's because of these men that I'm leaving this church.' Then he picked up his Bible and promptly left the church."

"No way!" *Now* I did look surprised.

"Yup," he said. "I was the assistant pastor at that time. That's how I became the pastor."

I let out a nervous laugh and said, "That didn't happen on that Sunday."

"Oh, *yes* it did," he defended. "I was there!"

"You may have been, but it *didn't happen **that** Sunday*." Now he was confused. I continued. "It may have come to a head that Sunday, but it happened *months* ... maybe *years* before when leadership began to tolerate broken relationships in the congregation. The seething anger of unresolved problems was stuffed underground, and people made it normal to live incongruently. No, it may have come to the surface that morning, but it had been *festering* for months."

He affirmed the observation and recounted several incidents where the wheels first began to slide.

When you have healthy relationships, people are genuinely excited to see each other. That ongoing sense of exuberance is observable to veterans as well as visitors. But when unresolved problems are tolerated, a sewer of unsettled offenses leaches a stench into the atmosphere.

Visitors detect it even though they might not be able to locate it.

Healthy relationships do not mean that problems never occur. **It simply means that when they do, we take the *time* and *effort* to resolve them.**

"We've got lots of problems," he emphasized. "How do you stop the problems?"

I explained with a metaphor. "My wife keeps a clean house. That doesn't mean our house never gets dirty. I have three kids! But it simply means that when it does get dirty, it doesn't stay that way for very long before it's cleaned up. Every healthy church that's growing has **one thing in common:** *problems*. The same is true with families and marriages. Problems often are signs that people are trying their best, for example, when people dance their feet often get tangled. But they don't quit there. They untangle and keep dancing!"

"Do you have a program for that?" he said. We both laughed.

"Here's one of the greatest benefits of all," I continued. "When healthy relationships are *present,* any program will work. But where personality conflicts and unresolved differences exist, no program will work regardless of how great it is. Hurting people have a tendency to sabotage each other's success. The program is inconsequential at this point-*wounded-ness* is."

"But can God heal our fellowship? It's been broken for so long," he lamented.

I took a deep breath and spoke, slowing to add *emphasis: "God is always faithful to bring healing, but you decide how long it will take."*

Several cups of coffee later, our conversation turned from diagnosis to remedy. "Here's what you should do. Go around to everyone you can, starting with your leaders, and ask them if there are ANY unresolved issues that need to be dealt with; accept no cordial denials. **Only honesty can bring contrition and forgiveness.** No more living with pretense. "In fact," I challenged him, "Maybe you should think of canceling your Sunday services until *everyone* has given each other a clean slate."

Now he looked more awake than I had seen him all morning. "What?" He looked offended. "Who are you to make such an outlandish request?"

"Oh, I'm sorry," I said. "Did I say that I was requesting it? How foolish. Forgive me for misleading you. I didn't request it. *Jesus did.*"

I took him to what Jesus said in Matthew 5:23-24:

Therefore if you are presenting your offering at the altar, and there remember that your brother has something against you, leave your offering there before the altar and go; first be reconciled to your brother, and then come and present your offering.[1]

I continued, "In other words, Jesus is saying that

having right relationships with one another is more important than having church."

He got the point. We said our good-byes, and for several months we kept in touch as the church went through a season of honesty and healing.

An *Encore Church* is marked by healthy relationships.

Churches are living organisms; they are not corporate organizations. They are active entities made up of living people, so the health of an *individual* affects the health of the *whole* church.

An *Encore Church* begins with the individual.

If an individual is fundamentally happy and healthy, barring any catastrophic accident he will seldom get sick. If he does, he doesn't stay sick very long. On the other hand, if that same person were under a weight of unresolved problems, anxieties, buried fears, and unsettled hurts; his immune system would be severely affected. He would become vulnerable to sickness and would soon surrender to illness. And when he did get sick, he would stay sick for a long time!

Churches are the same. When a culture of healthy relationships is compromised, we are at risk to a variety of diseases and we become predisposed to unnecessary relational illnesses. These illnesses include a lack of communication, a decrease in laughter, a diminishing joy, and an increase of gossip.

However, when relationships are *thriving,* our spiritual immune system *protects* us from random illnesses. Should we get ill, we are resilient and we heal quickly. This results in a tangible joy, camaraderie, and mutual support as people work together as a team.

*Now at this time Mary arose and went in a hurry
to the hill country, to a city of Judah, and entered the house
of Zacharias and greeted Elizabeth. When Elizabeth
heard Mary's greeting, the baby leaped in her womb;
and Elizabeth was filled with the Holy Spirit.*[2]
(Luke 1:39-41)

Mary and Elizabeth were more than cousins; they were friends. As soon as Mary found out that she was pregnant, she couldn't wait to tell Elizabeth. Even though the annunciation came from an angel and she knew there would be skeptics, she braved the long trek to the hill country. When Mary arrived and they greeted each other, Elizabeth who was also pregnant was filled with the Holy Spirit as her baby leaped within for joy.

Let me ask you a question: How did Elizabeth get filled with the Holy Spirit? Was it though a stirring evangelist? Did she attend a special revival meeting? Was it at a conference she attended?

It was none of the above. Rather, the Gift of heaven was imparted in the hug, an embrace, an excited

reunion between two friends. No special programs. No choirs performing. No impressive surroundings.

It happens all the time in **Encore Churches.** All that's required is healthy relationships. And it could be that during a routine greeting time, God's best miracles will occur.

IT'S TIME TO COLLECT FRIENDS

For the body is not one member, but many.[3]
(1 Corinthians 12:14)

In a society that resists closeness, healthy relationships offer a cure to loneliness. Genesis 2:18 reminds us: "The Lord God said, *'It is not good for the man to be alone.'*"[4]

We were created in such a way that apart from one

another, we cannot be fulfilled. Mother Teresa once said: *"If we have no peace, it is because we have forgotten that we belong to each other."*[5]

We can never forget that.

One of my dearest friends was a man named Noel Campbell. He is in his golden years now, but for several years, he was a mentor to me as I cut my teeth as a young upstart pastor.

At that time, "POG" collecting was the rage. These desirables were wax bottle caps with the moniker of a dairy imprinted on them. Aficionados of these collectibles predicted that POGs would surely out-value baseball cards one day.

Anticipating my new found wealth, I traded, bartered, and haggled with the best of them. Satisfied with my stash, I approached Noel one day and asked: "Noel, I'm about to get rich soon. So let me ask you … some collect baseball cards while others collect POGs. What are you collecting?" Noel's reply took me by surprise.

"I collect friends."

Have you ever heard another person say something perceptive and thought *I wish I would have said that?*

**Healthy relationships set the stage
for lifelong friendships.**

Under these conditions, friendships coalesce. The rest is secondary. Programs, facilities, resources, and organizational charts only begin to make sense in the context of healthy relationships.

ENCORE CHURCHES
IN OBSCURE SETTINGS

I have encountered *Encore Churches* in every shape and size. They can be found in prominent settings as well as in obscure ones. An *Encore Church* is found wherever people simply enjoy being with one another. There is no need for efficient agendas, impressive programs or expensive venues.

It was Sunday night during the middle of the winter. I was in a small church hall where they were celebrating the 75th birthday of one of their members. When congregants arrived, they greeted one another as if it were their first encounter after a long winter's hibernation. The setting was humble but everyone seemed *content*. Hot plates kept the hot things hot, and an ice-chest kept cold things cold. The carpet was worn from memories of past gatherings, and the bathrooms were … sufficient. It was colder than usual. The old wood stove wasn't able to keep pace with the size of the room, so most just kept their jackets buttoned.

But no one took notice of the surroundings. Instead, *laughter* periodically erupted from small, huddled groups as people traded *memories* throughout the evening. Then the pies came out from the kitchen. Oohs! Aahs! Mmms! let the bakers in the crowd know that they'd done good!

I will remember the unfettered candor that was absolutely refreshing. They didn't have much, but *good hearts* combined with a *good God* made those present feel as if they were the most *special* people on earth.

Those churches may not look all that impressive to some, **but they do to God.** There may have been Formica instead of granite and cement instead of hardwood, but this *Encore Church* helped me to realize that where healthy relationships exist, the Holy Spirit will be delighted to attend. He will be thrilled to fill the humblest surroundings with the presence of God.

Being diligent to preserve the unity of the Spirit in the bond of peace.[6]
(Ephesians 4:3)

ALWAYS LEARNING

*S*ome months ago during a question and answer session, a young man in his twenties raised his hand and asked, "How often have you made *major* mistakes in your life?"

My answer was: "On the average, about once **every week** since birth."

There was immediate laughter, but I interrupted, "However, the question is not whether or not you've *made* mistakes. The real question is: 'What have *you done* with those mistakes?'"

An *Encore Church* is comprised of people who are *constantly learning.*

Once you stop learning new things, you stop growing. The human spirit thrives on finding *new* discoveries about God, His will, about others, and ourselves. An old story is told about the Tatars, Bedouin sheepherders who traverse the deserts in search for pasture.

In order to survive, they must be ready to strike camp when their food source can no longer sustain their flocks, and they hunt for other desert watering holes and pastures for food.

They are a docile people who are mostly quiet and unassuming. However, on rare occasion when they get angry, a certain phrase to their opponent or antagonist sums it all up. Through pressed lips and red face, these stern words are heard: *"May you stay in one place the rest of your life!"*[1]

It seems tame at first glance, but understanding

the survival needs of the Tatar's herds and families, this would be the harshest curse that a desert dweller could bear.

New Hope is a church of young leaders who are still in the early stages of discovery, and one of the most common classrooms for growth is *trial-and-error.* Understanding this, we need to make room for both trials and errors.

We could have hired only veterans, but early on, we chose to be coaches, coaxing out potential from novices. Emerging leaders are a joy to work with. They keep you on your toes and on your knees at the same time! I am so glad that early on, we decided to develop young leaders rather than hire only veterans. I would do it all again, but there has come one great realization: *Inside every young leader are hundreds of mistakes just waiting to be made.*

Of course we are neither casual about errors nor are we cavalier about misjudgments. But we have to make adequate room for the young leader to find his way back if he has the fortitude to improve.

Martin Luther once said, "Love God and sin bold-ly!"[2]

He didn't say to sin *intentionally*. He simply meant that in our effort to love God, we will be prone to make mistakes. But if we are afraid of mistakes, we may not be able to love God fully.

Solomon said it wittingly: "Where no oxen are, the manger is clean, but much revenue comes by the strength of the ox."[3] (Proverbs 14:4). It was his way of saying that if your goal is a clean manger, you won't have any strength. But if you want strength, you'd better buy a shovel!

Errors in judgment, faults, and blunders are for the most part, not fatal. But what can be deadly is the way we deal with our failures. How we respond to them will determine the degree of damage that occurs.

So here is what I do. I squeeze every last drop of wisdom that mistakes will release to me. Then I throw the empty carcass of that over my shoulder and never think of it again. Mistakes deserve a *quick* funeral and a *slow* reflection.

Making a mistake gives you experience, but experience alone makes you none the wiser. Experience alone tells you that when you make the same mistake, you are immediately reminded that you've done this before!

It is not experience, but it is *reflection* that brings wisdom. Reflecting on the lessons from those mistakes brings improvement. The equation I often use is this:

Experience plus reflection equals insight.

NOTEBOOK LIVES

Some lives are like blank notebooks. They never write anything in them. No notations. No reflections. No experiences.

Others are like notebooks with experiences logged on each page. They make notations, but they are never reflected upon. They are never revisited. Their notebooks simply contain the records of past failures.

Others, however, spend time to *reflect* on the experiences. They *invest* in seasons, short and long, of solitude in order to consider what God is teaching. **It takes time and reflection to correct wrong perspectives and redefine life priorities.** These avid students of insight wring every bit of wisdom they can from the past, and they make deposits into the accounts from which great futures are built.

Experience without *reflection* can rush you toward *false conclusions*. It can cause you to become jaded and fearful to try again, leaving you to live cautiously involved rather than fully engaged. Mark Twain once said, "A cat that sits on a hot stove will not only never sit on a hot stove again; it won't sit on any stove!⁴

**A life of faith is based on action,
but a life of fear is based on the avoidance
of action.**

An *Encore Church* takes the time to reflect and, in doing so, learns.

One of the ways of reflecting on lessons is what we call *debriefing.* We debrief all the time! One characteristic of an *Encore Church's* culture is to build an environment of consistent learning by evaluating and debriefing. No, I didn't say criticizing and fault finding. It is learning and improving from the lessons learned.

Learning will begin with *us.* A healthy self-assessment will give us plenty to work on so we don't pick over the minutiae from other people's misdeeds so much. ***Building a heart to learn starts with checking ourselves.***

**Test yourselves to see if you are in the faith;
examine yourselves!**[5]
(2 Corinthians 13:5)

FEAR NOT THE TRUTH

Learning to face the truth, no matter how painful it might be, is one of the greatest principles for improving life. You cannot move forward unless you can be courageous enough to recognize truth.

If you cannot acknowledge that the job you have is the wrong one for you, you'll never be able to make the changes necessary. If you don't recognize that your marriage is struggling, you won't seek help or rectify the hurtful words that aggravate arguments. If you can't see the truth that you are overweight, you won't do what it takes to get rid of old habits that led to your obesity.

The truth will set you free; but first, it might make you miserable. But what is worse is holding onto falsehoods and denying the obvious.

I have found that we have a natural aversion to being corrected. It has become defined in our society that correction means personal failure.

Nothing could be further from the truth!

Instead, re-define correction as a discovery of *more potential that just got unearthed!* It's all about faith. You see, faith is seeing that there is more yet to come! Faith is seeing that our best days lay ahead of us, and there is more treasure yet to be discovered. Even though there are rivers yet to cross and mountains yet to climb, we can make the adjustments. And taking a cue off the old Star Trek narration, we can go where no man has gone before.

Problems will inevitably occur and denying them only makes for a certain future where problems slide underground. Instead, an *Encore Church* courageously confronts problems, but it also responds with mercy and grace. It doesn't expect to be a fair-weather church where problems are masked until the guilty are quietly removed.

Instead, an *Encore Church* is mature enough to recognize existing problems, but they are not viewed
as a movie critic would evaluate a screen plot. Instead, problems are confronted in the same way a
world-class group of surgeons would evaluate an
x-ray prior to surgery. The problem is discovered
and the way to best resolve it is agreed upon. The
surgeons don't berate the patient nor do they blame
genetics. Their goal is simply to rectify the trouble
and restore the patient to health.

Learning requires commitment, and it is commitment that can move mountains. An *Encore Church*
is not afraid of working hard. Remember the old
adage: *Mountain moving faith always carries a
pick.*

**Take the initiative to learn. Don't wait
until you are taught. Be curious.**

It was once said of John Wesley White that he could
listen any man's boring sermon into a spiritual
masterpiece. In other words, he put the responsibil-

ity of learning on himself and not on anyone else. Develop a hunger to learn fresh insights and experience new things. The human spirit thrives on learning and remember ... you can discover new truths from good teachers as well as bad!

One young leader returned from a two-month intensive session on apologetics at a university. I queried him upon his return. "How were the classes?" I asked.

"Half of them were good and half were bad," he replied.

"I don't understand. What do you mean?" I asked.

"Well," he said, "half the teachers were interesting so I learned from them. But the other teachers were boring, so I didn't learn from them."

"No!" I shouted trying to catch his attention. "You must *learn from the bad as well as the good.* If you just learn from the good, you will only learn half as

much. But if you learn from the bad as well, you'll learn twice as much!"

"How can you learn from the bad?" he retorted. "They bored me to death in the first three minutes."

"That's fantastic!" I said excitedly. "Do you know the kind of skill it takes to bore someone to death within three minutes? Find out what he's doing to accomplish that feat. Write it down! Was it his monotone voice? Maybe it was his lack of interest. Or could it have been a lack of passion? Find out whatever it was and you will know what *not* to do when you are asked to teach one day!"

Don't stop learning. Take the initiative to discover new truths ... about yourself and about God. Don't be afraid to dig deep. What you'll find will be the materials out of which great futures are made.

A poor yet wise lad is better than an old and foolish king who no longer knows how to receive instruction.[6]
(Ecclesiastes 4:13)

SELF-FEEDERS

*H*e looked haggard when he entered. "I think my season is up here," he said.

I leaned back in my chair and mused. "Why?"

"Well," he hesitated. "I'm just not being *fed* here."

I had heard those words before. Over my years as a senior minister, I've seen them come in and I've bid them adieu. But this one had me confused. "Not getting *fed?*" I pressed. "Tell me. Do you do your daily devotions?"

"I don't have time to," he shot back. "I'm too busy."

He had been with us for four years and if there's one drum that we beat on incessantly, it's doing daily devotions. So I was befuddled. I knew that this staff person had neglected one of the most important aspects of *genuine* Christian maturity.

"How old are you?" I asked.

"Twenty-eight."

"Oh, that's my son's age. Let me pose a scenario to you. What if he came to me one day, gaunt and emaciated. His eyes were sunken and his body was frail and his ribs were showing. Now let's say he looked at me with those depressed eyes and said, "I'm leaving this family."

"Why in the world are you doing that?" I would say.

"Because no one is feeding me around here anymore."

"What do you think my response would be?"

"Feed yourself!"

Feeding myself is no one else's responsibility but my own. I cannot expect others to feed me if I am to grow and mature. It is not the responsibility of a pastor, not an elder, not a Sunday School teacher. They will coach me, instruct me, encourage me, and sharpen my skills; but I alone am responsible to feed me!

The sixth mark of an *Encore Church* is that it is filled with self-feeders.

We often don't take the maintenance of our souls seriously until it is too late. I remember training for a long-distance race. My coach instructed me to hydrate at certain time intervals. "Every fifteen minutes," he told me, "drink six ounces of water. Keep an eye on the time so you don't violate your hydration limits."

"But coach, what if I am not thirsty?"

"Listen to me," he said with a serious stare. "If you wait until you're thirsty to take a drink, *it's too late.* Your body has already begun its slide into dehydration. You can't afford that."

For the past ten years, our staff and congregation have learned the discipline of feeding themselves on a daily basis. But for some reason, this staff person didn't feel it was necessary … until it was too late.

I accepted his resignation.

**But I remember a time when
I was in the same place.**

Shortly after I became a Christian, I remember complaining to God about the quality of my church's teaching. We had an academic-style preacher who often left me more confused than anything. I complained to God in the bathroom after a service.

"God!" I cried, hoping I was alone in the stall. "I'm going to *starve* in this place! I'm not getting fed. I'm *dying* here. I'm suffering from malnutrition!"

I'm not sure if it was a chuckle from the stall next to me or a reply from heaven, but I remember becoming acutely conscious of something as the Holy Spirit spoke to me from the depths of my own anguished being.

"What about Me?" came the gentle rebuke. *"Am I not enough.* If you intend to grow up, you must feed yourself."

I had been trying to live off a once-a-week feeding regimen; no wonder I was starving! What made matters worse was that I had resisted God's best program—His most gifted teacher, the Holy Spirit. He had been inviting me to be His student, but I remained unresponsive. Instead, I wanted others to do what only I could do ... take *responsibility* for my own spiritual health and nourishment.

The next day, I began a reading and journaling program that has been with me till this day. I have refined it of course, but the same heart and motive remains: I alone am answerable for my maturity and in order to grow, I have to *feed myself.* This experience resulted in what we have today as the *Life Journal* used by thousands of churches worldwide.

Be still, and know that I am God.[1]
(Psalms 46:10 NIV)

Solitude is the key to knowing God. It renews a fatigued heart. It is where a chafed soul goes to heal. Solitude provides the opportunity to scrub our souls and recalibrate life's compass. Without it, we can easily drift towards vanity.

Solitude differs from isolation. The latter happens when we violate the former. We then hunger to be left alone. We wait for the discontent to pass till we return neither empty nor filled.

Mother Teresa once said, "In order to keep a lamp burning, we have to keep putting oil in it.[2]

Sometimes I forget that. I am learning to take the time to maintain my heart.

STARTING POINTS

I have found that feeding myself has to be my starting point, at the beginning of my reach, not the end of it. It can't be something I struggle with. Should it ever become an option, my humanity would cast the deciding vote against it and I would quickly abandon the discipline.

> **Make me walk in the path of Your**
> **commandments, for I delight in it.**
> **Incline my heart to Your testimonies.[3]**
> (Psalms 119:35-36)

I remember at 24-years-old, I was a soccer coach at a nearby high school. This was more years ago than I care to admit, but at least I can still remember the lesson. Most of the players who came out for the team were motivated. Arriving on the first day of practice, they came to the field with a ball, shin guards, and soccer shoes.

One student, however, arrived with jeans and a backpack. Approaching me, he appeared more prepared for the debate team than for a scrimmage.

"I'm not sure whether I want to try out for soccer or band," he said. "They're both fun. What do you think, coach?"

"Well," I said slowly, "my job is to help you play better soccer, not help you make better decisions. Once your decision is made however, I can increase your skill level and teach you patterns of play; but until then, I am sort of on the sidelines. I expect you to arrive *already motivated* for the game; and if that is still in question, I can't coach you any further. My suggestion? *Try band.*"

Self-feeders motivate themselves to hear God on a daily basis. And when they arrive at the weekend services, sermons coach them further. **Self-feeders arrive coachable.**

In a recent edition of the *American Journal of Medicine,* doctors published a highly revealing conclusion:

The health of 21st century America will no longer be determined by what people can get the doctors to do for them. **The health of America today will be determined by what the doctors can get people *to do for themselves.*** [4]

Can you see how this prescription applies equally to each of us? A once-a-week meal, no matter how scrumptious, would in the long run, leave us weak and undernourished. But *daily meals* can change all of that. Regularly dining on the Word of God makes for stalwart, healthy saints—the only kind that will make a difference in this world.

**For it is not an idle word for you;
indeed it is your life. And by this word you
will prolong your days in the land, which you are
about to cross the Jordan to possess.**[5]
(Deuteronomy 32:47)

THE SHEPHERD'S HEART

It took place in a quaint white-washed country church during the Civil War. It had clapboard siding with a tall steeple, one like you'd see in a travel magazine or along a country dirt road.

It was to be the annual talent show a small community church had hosted for over twenty-five years. When the gathering began, people started volunteering one-by-one. The first was a little girl on a chair who presented her favorite memorized verse. A violin solo followed that squeaked in all the right places. Some sang; others recited poetry. Most stepped up willingly; others were nudged forward by volunteering friends.

As the evening progressed, the pastor began inviting the more reluctantly talented. In the middle pew was a tall, lanky man dressed with distinction in a dark suit. The pastor nodded toward Mr. Meriweather who everyone knew to be a seasoned actor, well-trained in Shakespeare. Stepping up front, he cleared his throat prompting everyone's attention. Then with sweeping gestures and a deep resonant voice, the shepherd's psalm echoed through the chapel.

"The Lor-dah is my shepherd! I shall not want … "[6]

He recited the classic psalm with masterful poise and flattering eloquence. He concluded to the brisk applause of a thrilled audience.

The pastor let a moment pass as a brief afterglow ensued. After a minute or two, the pastor turned to a frail farmer from down the road. "Joseph, would you be next?" the pastor urged.

"Aw shucks," the farmer replied. "I don't know nuthin'."

"Sure you do!" the pastor wheedled. "Come on up, Joseph!"

Others joined in the coaxing until sheer embarrassment forced him forward. Fidgeting from side-to-side, he half mumbled, "Shucks, I don't know much; but I was gonna share the same verse as Mr. Meriweather, but he already done said it all."

"Share it again!" the pastor encouraged, and soon others were echoing the request.

Joseph was in his early sixties and had been born and raised in the country. He had a simple background of subsistence farming. Hard times had fallen on his little farm but he remained a godly and soft-spoken, a man who never complained.

Swallowing hard, he stammered and started again. "The Lord is my Shepherd and 'cause of that one thing, I figure I have everything I need."

Then detouring on a side route, he continued. "Y'all know that momma died six years ago. I didn't think I could go on without her. But God never left me and He reminded me that I was gonna do just *fine*. He said He'd be there for the kids and me, and He was." He paused to find his place and then he continued. "He makes me lie down in green pastures. He leads me beside still streams. He restores my soul. He leads me … "

Joseph's thoughts were interrupted by yet another remembrance.

"Y'all know that during the war, my boys felt it right to join up. The day they left was the last day I saw them. I run the farm alone now … No, I guess not alone. He restored my soul that following year. It didn't come easily, but *God's never late*. He goes before me now and prepares my table. And when I don't think I have much left, my cup always overflows."

He took the congregation down the scenic path of the Good Shepherd, one that Joseph himself had followed many times before. He concluded the 23rd Psalm:

"Surely goodness and mercy will follow me and I look forward to dwelling in the house of the Lord, and I know it will be my home too, and momma's ... forever."

Without anyone noticing, a deep silence had filled the room; the kind when someone very important dies or when a deep respect is the only response you can give. It's the silence when you don't know what to do, so you just don't do anything at all. Joseph sat down and no one moved.

Slowly, Mr. Meriweather made his way to the front. Standing for a moment as if to find words appropriate enough to disturb the silence, he spoke:

**"I may know the shepherd's psalm ... but Joseph?
He knows the Shepherd,
and that makes all the difference."**

*Feed on God's Word. It will help you know the
Shepherd intimately.*

Knowing about God and knowing Him personally
are galaxies apart. One might bring notoriety, but
the other brings *depth*. Recognize the difference
and choose well.

That one decision will make all the difference.

*God sees not as man sees, for man looks at the
outward appearance, but the Lord looks at the heart.*[7]
(1 Samuel 16:7)

CONNECT EVERYTHING
TO A SOUL

*H*eaven holds sights and sounds in store for us that will astound even our wildest imaginations and keep us overwhelmed for eternity. I can't wait to talk with King David in person or walk with Enoch. I want to meet the archangels, Michael and Gabriel, and see how God created the heavens: Orion to Pleiades, from a supernova to the Aurora Borealis.

For the first million years or so, we'll be star struck and suspended in amazement by all those things that take our breath away. We'll be mesmerized by the streets of gold, the cherubim, seraphim and the

saints of old. And I'm sure we'll spend years trying to find the street address to the mansion that
belongs to us.

But what will make our hearts beat out of our
chests will be when the clouds roll back, and a
trumpet blast splits the heavens. The Lamb of God
will rise to the shouts and cries of the millions who
have been redeemed. The Promised One will step
through a stellar explosion that will cause even angels to shield their eyes from the brilliance.

I remember the old hymn whose verses ring:

> **"When we all get to heaven,**
> **what a day of rejoicing that will be!**
> **When we all see Jesus,**
> **we'll sing and shout the victory!"**[1]

We'll see so many breathtaking sights and magnifi-
cent scenes that it will take us centuries to even get
past the initial sensation. But of all the trillions of
surprises, there's *one* thing we will *never* see again
for all of eternity.

We will never see another non-Christian.

Right now, in this life, we have the only opportunity to usher people to the Forgiver. Our lifetime contains the only possibility for us personally to be part of God's plan. We have been invited to partner with the Redeemer to present the good news in creative ways to those who need Him the most.

An Encore Church connects everything it does to a soul.

The harvest won't self-reap, but it will self-destruct if not reaped. Early on, we decided to be a harvest church. And of all the noble activities we could be involved in, we wanted to be known for one thing: helping people find their way back to the Savior.

Behold, I say to you, lift up your eyes and look on the fields, that they are white for harvest.[2]
(John 4:35)

We may not be the best at hosting social events, church conferences, or for having huge buildings with impressive budgets. But in the end what matters the most will be souls that have been redeemed. So we connect everything to a soul without apology.

In the early years of New Hope, I remember talking with one of our wonderful volunteers who arrived early that morning. In those days, our loud speakers were attached to stands. The speakers were then manually raised to an appropriate height so the sound could be projected over the heads of the congregation for optimum dispersion.

Just as the volunteer was completing the task, I posed the question. "What are you doing?" I asked.

"I'm setting up a speaker."

"No, you're not," I replied.

"Oh, yes I am," he said. "I've been doing this each week for six months."

"But you're not," I pushed back.

Quizzically he turned to me and said, "OK, just what am I doing, Pastor?"

I said, "You are making it possible for a new person to *hear* the gospel *clearly* and without distraction probably for the first time in his life. Because of your efforts here, when that person responds to Christ positively ... when that person lifts his hand to say "Yes" to God's offer of forgiveness and salvation, we will rejoice together. Why? Because I didn't lead him to Christ ...

"We did it together!"

I held out my hand and said, "Thank you."

I left the auditorium and walked over to our children's section. There I found a young lady from our Pacific Rim Bible College. She was volunteering in the nursery as part of her work-study program.

"What are you doing?" I asked.

"Why, I'm changing a diaper," she replied. She studied me for a moment as if she were thinking, "with a minimum of observation skills anyone can recognize what I am doing!"

Suspecting what she was thinking, I pressed forward. *"No, you're not,"* I replied.

"Oh, yes I am!" she insisted, wrinkling her nose.

"Nope," I said.

"Then you tell me, Pastor, just what am I doing," she said with a wry smile, knowing something was up but not quite knowing what.

"You are making it possible for a young mother to entrust her child into the care of another. And because of that, she is able to listen to the gospel without being distracted by the constant needs of her youngster. At the end of the service when she

opens her heart to God, I didn't lead her to Christ
…

"We did it together."

I held out my hand and said, "Thank you."

The outreaches, picnics, camps, and weekend services we plan are not ends in themselves. They are a means to something far more eternal. We can never miss that purpose and think that our role is to convince the already convinced over and again.

I think that when the day comes for me to stand before His throne one day in heaven, He will ask me one specific question. He will not ask me how big our choir was. He won't ask how popular our potlucks were nor will He ask the size and budget of our building program. He will ask one important question:

"How many of my children did you bring home with you?"

Now is our time. We won't have another chance at this life again. This is our run.

An *Encore Church* never forgets her assignment. Our energies, our activities, our planning, and our actions are somehow, somewhere ... to be connected to a soul.

Several years ago, a friend of mine related this story of his college years. His final exam required the completion of a certain book report that would hold 50% of his grade. He worked long and hard on this assignment, completed it and turned it in. Several days later, he received it back. Conspicuously on the front cover, in bold red ink, were these words:

"Great art work! Excellent bibliography! Outstanding research! Grade: 'F.' Wrong assignment!"

When he told me his story, it took me two days to stop laughing. For weeks I would chuckle whenever it came back to my mind.

I wonder if God will say that to numerous churches on that day: "Great building, nice potlucks, great Bible study groups … 'F' …
Wrong assignment!"

We have one life to give, and if we will model our assignment after His, we won't be too far off!

Jesus said to them again …
"as the Father has sent Me, I also send you."[3]
(John 20:21)

A CHOSEN LOVE

J guess you might call me biased.

I come from a long lineage that amalgamates the Portuguese, Japanese, and Hawaiian ancestries.

My great-grandfather was a *luna*, or a foreman, on the Parker Ranch in Waimea where Anna and I planted a church in 1991. We only have a black-and-white photograph of him in his plaid-print *palaka shirt* that was the typical wear of the ranch hands we knew as *paniolo*.

Anna and I would leave from Hilo on Sunday after-noons and drive along the Hamakua coastline. Our services in Waimea were held on Sunday evenings for nearly two years until we installed a full-time pastor.

I remember the sweet smell of the freshly harvest-ed sugar cane that was thick in the humid air. On the infrequent sunnier days, I would ride my mo-torcycle through patches of pungent ginger grow-ing wild along the roadway. A lingering gauntlet of fragrance would scent the air for miles. Now years later, these memories still accompany me as I travel down the same highway.

Hawaii's fresh floral air energizes you. Its breath-taking, natural beauty renews you, but the most unique feature that brings you back is ... *the people.*

The warmth of the Aloha spirit in the islanders wonderfully complements the islands' perfect temperatures. A unique blend of nationalities and languages create a distinctive flavor all its own as East and West merge to propagate some of the most beautiful children on the globe. A delightful intermingling of ethnicities, we live together as `ohana.

I have come to love the people of these islands, but that love came by *choice*. I received my education and early experience in ministry in the Northwest, but we chose to move back twenty-five years ago. Many reasons argued against our homeward move, but it was a love for the island people that compelled us.

An *Encore Church* chooses to love the people in its community and its calling to reach them.

The greatest love is a love of choice. The Bible calls it *agape*. No other quality of love will be sufficient for the long haul.

STRENGTH FOR THE JOURNEY

I recall a cross-country coach who instilled in me the love for running many years ago. (I will have to admit that since then, my love has somewhat flagged a bit!) But nevertheless, I asked him what the priority needs were in order to run great races.

"Should I purchase good shoes? Or maybe I can pick up a nice pair of silk running shorts. Or what about a sport watch with multiple functions?"

"It's none of the above," he said. "Your first priority is simply this: learn to love running. Enjoy the outdoors. Pace the early morning sunrise or run into the evening's sunset. Breathe in the fresh air. Take a detour through a park you've never visited and watch children play. When you run to win, you'll soon get tired of it." Then he finished with this:

"But when you run simply because you love running, you'll run forever."

LOVE IS THE ONLY REASON

**Moved with compassion,
Jesus touched their eyes; and immediately they
regained their sight and followed Him.**[1]
(Matthew 20:34)

Several times in the New Testament we find what compelled Jesus to issue a miracle. He was *moved with compassion.* No other reason and no other motive. He still operates on the same principle today.

Miracles are usually prefaced by compassion. Without it, we are striving for something divine in order to increase our personal goals rather than making room for His.

I received a call one day from a man who was considering relocating to Hawaii to start a new church. We set a time to meet for breakfast at one of our local hangouts, Sam Choy's on Nimitz Highway.

We sat down and ordered off the menu. I had my favorite: Portuguese sausage, eggs and rice. He had oatmeal. I guess I should have too, but my diet didn't begin until *tomorrow*.

We exchanged a few pleasantries and then he began.

"I serve with a denomination that has no representative church to date in these islands. They are willing to invest several thousands of dollars to get one started, and they've asked me to move here and lead it. What do you think?"

"That was sure nice of them to be so willing to invest so much money in a new church plant!" I replied. "Do you love the Asian and Polynesian people?"

"Oh, they've been given the nicest place on the globe to live, haven't they? You can't beat Hawaii! And my kids love the beaches."

"I agree wholeheartedly!" I said. Then I repeated, *"But can you love the people?"*

"Yes, the people here are so blessed to have such nice weather all year long. Why where I come from, we just hunker down for six months a year waiting for spring to arrive!"

Still I wasn't sure he understood my question, so I again repeated: "But *do you love the people here* more than any other on the face of the earth? Is this your last whistle stop or is it another point in your journey onward?"

"What do you mean?" he replied.

"The people here are precious and they deserve to be loved deeply. Do you know their customs? Do you know the history of the islands? Did you know they take naps in the park and sometimes stop in the middle of the street to talk story with a friend they haven't seen in a while? Do you like *Kim Chee?* What about *poi?* Have you ever tasted haupia? Would you be willing to try some *lumpia?"*

He stared at me as if I were speaking a foreign language.

"I'm sure I will like their food. We have a Chinese restaurant in my Mainland hometown that we eat at sometimes."

I smiled and said, "*We really don't need another church here.*"

He gave me an incredulous look that made me hasten to my next point. "*But we can use many more Christian leaders who will choose to love Hawaii's people.*"

I continued.

"Here's my take, for what it's worth: Don't start a church just yet. First, put up a map of Hawaii on your wall and pray over the towns; walk down the avenues and learn how to pronounce the street names. Take some time to get to know the people. Learn to love them for who they are. Love the foods they eat, the customs they practice, and the way they live.

The only reason to come to Hawaii must be to love the people in Christ's name; not for a job, not to fulfill a denomination's expectations, not for the weather.

But if you'll come to love them, they'll come to love you."

My advice was too little—too late. The gears had already been in motion and he moved in two months to Hawaii. He did his best to comply with his denomination's request. However, three years later, the doors of the fledgling church were shut, and the pastor used the second leg of his roundtrip ticket.

LOVE TRANSFORMS

Genuine love constantly monitors our hearts and checks our motives. It governs our actions and prunes what is hollow.

It transforms what we believe into how we live. It closes the gap of inconsistency and holds us firmly accountable to live what we believe.

Several years ago, I received one of the best letters ever. It was sent anonymously, and although I may never know the author, I will always be grateful for their gift. It is framed in my office and reminds me daily that love converts a belief into a conviction and it transports what's in my heart to what's in my shoes.

Here's an excerpt of the letter:

When you asked Jesus into your heart,
*   you invested in me.*
When you answered "Yes" to the call,
*   you invested in me.*
When you decided to be loyal to Anna,
*   you invested in me.*
When you let God make victories out of your defeats,
*   you invested in me.*
When you received God's Word as God's Word and

started the Life Journal,
>*you invested in me.*
When you refused to compromise,
>*you invested in me.*

Funny, I've known you for less than a year, but for over three decades, you have loved me by investing in me! And for all the "me's" in the Church around the world, thank you for continuing to give your life. Please don't stop. You are showing each of us how to do the same.

I am finding the older I get, the more I want to do only the things I love to do. That doesn't mean I do little or that I am picky. It simply means that I want to pour more heart into everything I do. Every other motive leaves me shallow and fatigued.

Mother Teresa who has mentored me from afar through her books, once said: "It is not the magnitude of our actions but the amount of love that is put into them that matters."[2]

When I do things out of a heart of love, I am filled and even small things become big.

Love is the most consistent monitor of hearts. It doesn't guarantee mistakes will not be made. It will not assure that toes will not be stepped on. But it will promise that God's hand will remain steady on our life, and that He will be glad to show up in delightful ways.

An *Encore Church* chooses that above everything else.

For the love of Christ controls us, having concluded this, that one died for all, therefore all died.[3]
(2 Corinthians 5:14)

A FINAL WORD

That He might present to Himself the church in all her glory,
having no spot or wrinkle or any such thing;
but that she would be holy and blameless.[1]
(Ephesians 5:27)

hus ends the eight marks of an *Encore Church*. While each quality deserves a book all its own, the compilation of these eight together helps to better define a picture-perfect Bride. As the Church, we still have a long way to go, but making progress toward that is enough to cause His heart to leap with delight.

The ones mentioned in this book are not simply

points of evaluation; defining them as such may cast a discouraging shadow. Instead they have been intended to bring fresh aspiration to our hearts. These markings are available to any person or church hungry for the gladness of God.

And for those who will choose and cultivate these, they will hear the applause of heaven and see the angels rise together to shout ...

"Encore!"

ENDNOTES

Chapter 1

1. See Rabbi Noah Weinberg, *5 Levels of Pleasure,* (New York: Select Books)
2. Psalm 98:8
3. Matthew 6:22–23
4. See Lewis Lockwood, Beethoven: *The Music and the Life,* (New York: W. W. Norton & Company, Inc.)
5. Eph 1:18–19

Chapter 2

1. See Malcolm Muggeridge, *Something Beautiful for God: Mother Teresa of Calcutta,* (New York: Harper Collins Publishers)
2. Proverbs 4:23

Chapter 3

1. Deuteronomy 28:2
2. See Eifion Evans, *The Welsh Revival of 1904,* (United Kingdom: Bryntirion Press)

3. See William Jennings Bryan (Editor-in-Chief), Francis W. Halsey (Associate Editor), *The World's Famous Orations Vol IX,* (New York, Funk and Wagnalls Company)
4. Matthew 18:20
5. Zepheniah 3:17

Chapter 4

1. Matthew 5:23–24
2. Luke 1:39–41
3. 1 Corinthians 12:14
4. Genesis 2:18
5. See Mother Theresa, *Mother Teresa: In My Own Words,* (New York: Gramercy Books a division of Random House Value Publishing)
6. Ephesians 4:3

Chapter 5

1. See Anne Blunt, Wilfrid Scawen Blunt, *Bedouin Tribes of the Euphrates,* New York: Harper & Brothers Publishing, 1879)
2. See Martin Luther and John Dillenberger, *Martin Luther: Selections From His Writings,* (New York: DoubleDay)
3. Proverbs 14:4
4. See Mark Twain, *Mark Twain: Collected Tales, Sketches, Speeches, and Essays: Vol: 2 (1891-1910)* (New York: Library of America, Penguin Putnam Inc.)
5. 2 Corinthians 13:5
6. Ecclesiastes 4:13

Chapter 6
1.   Psalm 46:10 (NIV)
2.   See Malcolm Muggeridge, *Something Beautiful for God:*
     Mother Teresa of Calcutta, (New York: HarperCollins
     Publishers)
3.   Psalm 119:35–36
4.   See The American Journal of Medice
     (New York: Thomson Reuters)
5.   Deuteronomy 32:47
6.   Psalm 23
7.   1 Samuel 16:7

Chapter 7
1.   See hymn by Eliza E. Hewitt, *When We all Get to Heaven,*
     (Public Domain)
2.   John 4:35
3.   John 20:21

Chapter 8
1.   Matthew 20:34
2.   See Malcolm Muggeridge, *Something Beautiful for God:*
     Mother Teresa of Calcutta, (New York: HarperCollins
     Publishers)
3.   2 Corinthians 5:14

A Final Word
1.   Ephesians 5:27

It was a balmy California evening. I had gone for a jog before I was to speak at a leadership conference. I still can't recall how I got there, but I found myself sitting on a curb weeping uncontrollably. I couldn't tell if it took place suddenly or gradually, but I knew something had broken inside. I remember lifting my trembling hands and asking out loud, "What in the world is happening to me?"

I had been leading on empty. That incident began a three-year odyssey I could never have imagined.

Are You Leading on Empty? If you're a church or ministry leader, you probably identify with Wayne Cordeiro's experience of being overwhelmed by the demands of ministry. At times you may find yourself depleted of energy and longing to escape the constant pressure.

In Leading on Empty, *Wayne Cordeiro candidly shares* his experience with the hope that it will encourage others headed down the same path. He was able to get back in touch with his life, get back in proper balance, and allow God to reenergize his spirit in a way that propelled him forward to greater levels of service. Learn from his experience how you can continue a fruitful ministry.

Better yet, take advantage of Wayne's helpful advice early on and avoid burnout altogether.

Don't Let **Burnout** *Get the Best of You!*

WAYNE CORDEIRO
AUTHOR OF THE DIVINE MENTOR

LEADING ON EMPTY
REFILLING YOUR TANK AND RENEWING YOUR PASSION

Life Resources

Capture God's promises as well as the counsel of divine mentors as you meet with them in your daily devotions.

The "Life Calendar" is designed to prompt you to obedience in the area of prayer, relationships and life essentials. This tool will help you become all you were meant to be!

JOURNALING is an excellent way to both record and process what God says. It's also a useful tool to use at a later time, to reflect on and review some of the 'gems' that you have received. Without writing them down, you may forget those blessings and some very important life lessons!

Each journal contains a Table of Contents, Prayer List, Daily Pages and the Bible Reading Plan for accountability, discipline and for systematic instruction on God's Word.

For a FREE CATALOG or for more information, check out **www.lifejournal.cc**

MORE OF THE BEST
FROM WAYNE CORDEIRO

The Dream Releasers How to Help Others Realize Their Dreams While Achieving Your Own
The Seven Rules of Success Indispensible Wisdom for Life
Attitudes That Attract Success You're Only One Attitude Away from a GREAT Life!
Doing Church As A Team The Miracle of Teamwork and How It Transforms Churches
Culture Shift Transforming Your Church from the Inside Out

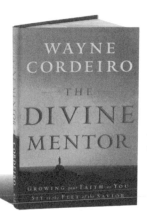

The Divine Mentor
Growing Your Faith as You Sit at the Feet of your Savior

For a FREE CATALOG or for more information, check out **www.lifejournal.cc**